IPHIGENIA AT TAURIS

Euripides
adapted into English verse by
Brian Vinero

BROADWAY PLAY PUBLISHING INC
New York
www.broadwayplaypublishing.com
info@broadwayplaypublishing.com

Cover art: Iphigenia, fresco from House of Lucius Caecilius Jucundus in Pompeii

First edition: January 2025
I S B N: 979-8-88856-027-3

Book design: Marie Donovan
Page make-up: Adobe InDesign
Typeface: Palatino

TRANSLATOR'S NOTES

Greek tragedy is not for the faint of heart. It is a tremendous challenge for actors and audiences, and yes, for the translator. These plays are not a slice-of-life or a character study. They tend to unfold on the worst day of the protagonist's life. The characters face insurmountable odds, callous cruelty and horrors in a tangled web of misery that only one of the Greek Gods can untangle. We collectively hold our breath for the deus ex machina when a force beyond the power of mere mortals will set things right.

A classic Greek drama was not meant to be subtle. It was akin to a religious ritual performed in a grand, outdoor cathedral where the sky itself was the dome. And the actors wore masks that did not allow for the subtlety that a small-scale contemporary play or a movie camera allows. The imagery and emotions in the dialogue were required to go beyond words and become poetry that could penetrate the ears of well over a thousand observers who would only experience the play once during an annual festival. The plays utilized rhyme which helped the spectators hear, but also helped the actors memorize mammoth speeches some of which are three times the length of a typical Shakespearean soliloquy. A highly-trained chorus used music and movement to take the audience along on a journey unaided by modern stagecraft's use of lighting and scenery.

While there have been many adaptations of the works of Euripides in English, I believe that placing them in rhymed verse in iambic pentameter is the most effective way to create an approximation of the original Greek verse in our language. This form is familiar to classically trained English-speaking actors who have studied the works of Shakespeare and his contemporaries. By heightening the language it creates a structure which allows the actor to create the larger-than-life truth that is required in classical acting. The measured rhythm of iambic pentameter is a heartbeat which can help keep the actors on track while performing a very challenging play, particularly during lengthy scenes and speeches.

I have crafted this translation with the intent of having it used for performance. While I have strongly endeavored to remain true to Euripides' dramatic intent, philosophy and imagery, I have not been slavishly faithful in the dialogue. In particular when he uses a colloquial phrase or makes a reference to a person or event in Greek history or mythology that would be clear to an Athenian audience of his time it could be all but incomprehensible to a contemporary audience. I have traded the pursuit of a literal word-for-word adaptation for a work respectful of the poetry and dramatic intensity of this Greek tragedy. To this end the choral passages are presented as lyrical interludes to the dialogue which is structured within the poetic language of rhymed verse.

The fall of the House of Atreus can be seen as the most relatable tale to come from the Trojan War. In our era we will never have to travel across the sea to avoid the wrath of an angry god, fire an arrow into a demigod's heel, or fight a Cyclops. Still, we certainly can understand the complex family dynamics where pride and anger send an act of infidelity spiraling into an all-out bloodbath that will transform a once-noble house forever. Aeschylus, Euripides' competitor in the annual Dionysia, won acclaim for his *Oresteia*, which recounted much of this story in his plays AGAMEMNON, THE LIBATION BEARERS and THE EUMENIDES. The only extant example we have of Greek Tragedy crafted into a trilogy, the *Oresteia* won Aeschylus First Prize at the Dionysia in 458 B.C. and stands as his best-known work today.

Euripides also created drama from the fate of this cursed family as did Sophocles. Written over an approximately fifteen year period, Euripides unfolded his narrative in four plays, not in chronological order, with the play recounting the dawn of the war, IPHIGENIA AT AULIS, written last and generally regarded as left incomplete at his death. The dramatic arc covering the fall of the House of Atreus before, during, and after the Trojan War focusing on the children of Agamemnon can be followed by reading Euripides' plays in this order: IPHIGENIA AT AULIS, ELECTRA, ORESTES and IPHIGENIA AT TAURIS. During my endeavors to adapt all of the works of Euripides into rhymed English verse, it has occurred to me that these plays create a more than worthy alternative to the *Oresteia*. Other works that have survived antiquity may also display the grandiosity, poetry, and ritual similar to what Euripides offers, but few playwrights of any era can equal his insight into human nature and the depth of his philosophical discourse. I don't hesitate to assert that time has proven Euripides to be the greatest of the Greek Tragedians.

In these four interconnected narratives, Iphigenia's fate is used as bookends. Her status as the favorite child of both parents, Agamemnon and Clytemnestra, will not be enough to forestall her fate as a pawn, helpless against the rising tide of politics and war. Euripides may or may not have been conscious that his two Iphigenia plays serve as mirror images of each other: In IPHIGENIA AT AULIS, she begins as a young girl on what she believes is a day of joy at the seashore and ends resigned to a gruesome fate as a sacrifice. In IPHIGENIA AT TAURIS, we find a woman hardened by time, trapped in a place of little hope with the bloody markings of death and human sacrifice surrounding her. But by the end of the play, she has found hope and freedom as the seashore becomes a portal to return her to her homeland and what remains of her family.

While all of Euripides' extant plays besides the satirical CYCLOPS are dramas and usually labeled as "Greek Tragedy," this play, (as with ALCESTIS, ION, and HELEN), has a hopeful ending and seems to have more in common with what today we might classify as a "romance." Euripides was known for being a rule breaker and taking liberties with established theatrical norms, which may have cost him quite a few First Place finishes at the Dionysia. His use of innovative plot devices and narrative twists such as mistaken identity and dramatic irony are on display in IPHIGENIA AT TAURIS. The example of such innovations would prove to be essential as the craft of playwrighting became more complex and sophisticated over time.

Indeed, this tale of long-lost siblings finding each other via happenstance in a foreign locale many years after being separated would be at home in a Nineteenth Century melodrama. However, with the grandiosity provided by the presence of the Gods and the stark setting of a mysterious temple, Euripides keeps the play firmly planted in high seriousness, assuring that the dramatic does not devolve into the melodramatic. Though the ending is optimistic and seemingly happy, the relief we may feel cannot counteract the despair and tragedy we know these siblings have weathered over a time of war and upheaval that has destroyed their family, which now bears an indelible stain from this endless bloodbath. Being of the noble class, they are trapped between the world of typical mortals and the powerful Gods that rule their world. Being elevated among mortals makes them the most obvious choice as playthings of the Gods, who can prove petty and treacherous and will make certain that nothing comes easy for the descendants of Atreus. But from Attic Tragedy to Shakespeare to *Succession*, a playwright knows that the trials and tribulations of the noble and powerful makes for great drama.

IPHIGENIA AT TAURIS can be seen as epilogue to the iconic events that precede it, while also standing alone as a tight story of suspense. With Iphigenia, Euripides once again provides actresses with a central, challenging, role of great power and nuance, which is one of many reasons I hope theatre makers will allow audiences rediscover this work of a master playwright working at the peak of his powers.

ACKNOWLEDGMENTS

I wish to express my thanks to Erik Schark for his
editorial support on this and many of my other projects
while doing double duty as the finest actor I know.
I would also like to acknowledge my friends and
colleagues who have held my hand as it "held the
quill" during the long and daunting task of crafting
a play written in a foreign language into rhymed,
English verse; in particular: Linda Johnson-Tomsho,
Melinda Brickhouse, Zach Curtis, Jim Miles, Dawn
Baker, Aaron Shelbrack, Shirley Mier, Paul Lavrakas,
Steven Kennedy, Eric Rockwell and my fellow
playwrights Stephen Cole, Rus McCoy and James
Harris. I am also greatly appreciative of the support I
have received from Marta Praeger and the staff at the
Robert A. Freedman Dramatic Agency.

DEDICATION

For the wonderful and resourceful theatre artist Aaron Kahn. It has been a long journey.

CHARACTERS & SETTING

IPHIGENIA, *a priestess of Artemis*
ORESTES, *her brother*
PYLADES, *kinsman of* ORESTES
HERDSMAN, *a Taurian peasant*
THOAS, *King of the Taurians*
MESSENGER, *servant to* THOAS
ATHENA, *Goddess of Wisdom*

CHORUS OF GREEK WOMEN
ATTENDANTS *to* THOAS

The action takes place in front of the temple of Artemis in Tauris.

(We are in front of the temple of Artemis in Tauris.
IPHIGENIA *enters.)*

IPHIGENIA:

A family line runs through the blood, and we
Cannot control the ebb and flow. The sea,
A river, it is all the same. We are
The children of the crests and tides. And far
Beyond all graves and tombs we seek to see
And understand our fate and destiny.
Great men have drawn a line that led me here,
Great kings from far across the sea, yet near.
When I recall the stories I was told
Of Tantalus, a king in days of old,
Who bore a son named Pelops who would ride
The fastest, swiftest steeds. He took a bride,
The daughter of King Oenomaus, and they
Brought forth a son who would be king one day,
My grandfather, King Atreus, who would
Bring forth two sons. First Menelaus stood
Beside him at the throne. Then one day came
Forth Agamemnon. Yes, the man whose name
Would ring from sea to mountain. And then I
Was born to Agamemnon, carried by
His consort Clytemnestra, daughter to
Tyndareus. My father followed through
A bargain struck with Artemis and made
A sacrifice of me and held the blade
Himself. And all because of Helen. One
Dark day in Aulis, where the sea is spun
Within great gusts of wind, he gathered men

Together crying vengeance, hoping then
To cross the sea to Troy, retrieving she
Who fled a husband's home and arms. The sea
Was waiting for a thousand ships to take
Ten thousand men to Troy, all for the sake
Of Menelaus. But there was no breath
Of wind upon a sea as still as death.
There was a seer Calchas who then said
A sacrifice was needed. So they spread
Out wood and grass for burning, and the dust
And smoke then billowed all around, and just
Then Calchas spoke his darkest prophecy:
He said to send these ships across the sea,
True sacrifice will be required of
Our leader Agamemnon. What you love
And treasure, your sweet daughter, now must bleed
Upon these rocks to see the wind is freed.
A sacrifice to Artemis is due,
A sacrifice that now must come from you.
You must relinquish something precious now,
A payment for a long-forgotten vow
And for great crimes both past and present. You
Brought forth a lovely daughter. Give her to
The darkness. And Odysseus then spun
A tale to take me from my mother. One
Brief moment I believed I would be wed
And handed to Achilles, but instead
They handed me off to an army. They
Were calling for my blood before the day
Was done. The sword was raised before me. I
Was there upon the altar. Then the sky
Blinked open, then before me, standing there,
The Goddess Artemis herself. And where
I lay there ready for the slaughter she
Replaced me with a deer so rapidly
That no man present noticed. Then the sky
Blinked open once again and let me fly

Away with her to safety far away
To here among the Taurians, though they
Are quite barbaric, ruled by Thoas, who
Is quite beyond barbaric. And I do
The bidding of the Goddess who brought me
To safety, and I labor willingly,
Devoted to her as her priestess. I
Take great responsibility in my
Most-sacred duties to her, but they are
Unspeakable to some and truly far
Beyond what many would consider kind,
But I will not reveal them. Should she find
Out I spoke of the sacred secrets, she
Might then respond in anger. I must be
Prepared to sacrifice my countrymen
Who dare to step upon this land. Back when
This city first was settled, there was law,
A law that has not changed. But I don't draw
The blood myself. My duty is to see
They are prepared for sacrifice. They'll be
Both shaved and cleansed. Then someone else will send
Them off to Hades. But what will portend
Of visions that the night revealed? I will
Just tell it to the air and sky to still
My beating heart. Last night I dreamed that I
Was whisked back home to Argos, there in my
Bedchamber built for maidens. Suddenly
The ground began to rumble angrily.
I ran outside in terror, and just then
The House of Atreus was crumbling. When
The pillars shook, the roof collapsed, but there
Remained one pillar standing like a dare.
But still the home of all my fathers gone
As if a body broken. But then on
The top of all the rubble it seemed hair
Was growing like a man's, and then I swear

I heard a voice and knew what I must do.
So I prepared it for its death and drew
Up holy water. Then I sprinkled it
Upon the wreckage hoping to commit
This sacrifice to peaceful death. So I
Interpret this foul dream is saying my
Poor brother is now dead. Orestes was
The pillar of the house that fell. Because
The sons support the name, and that is all
That will remain if pillars dare to fall.
I purified him. That's a sign that he
Is dead. There is no other who would be
Within my dreams. So I must seek to try
Now that I am awake to show him I
Will mourn for him though I am far away
And will perform a ritual today
To consecrate the dead. These sacred walls
Contain my countrywomen. Hear my calls,
My sisters bound to me, or must I go
Within these sacred rooms that house us? Know
The King has given you a duty, and
It's time to start the ritual I planned.

(IPHIGENIA *exits within the temple.* ORESTES *and* PYLADES
enter stealthily.)

ORESTES:
Take care and see if anyone is there.

PYLADES:
My eyes are sharp and looking everywhere.

ORESTES:
Then Pylades do you believe we are
At least within the temple that is our
Intended destination? We have sailed
A sea from Argos seeking it.

PYLADES:
And scaled

Great stones to find this sacred place. And I
Believe, as you should too, we're here.

ORESTES:

I spy
An altar dripping red with blood, do you?
And I believe the blood is Greek.

PYLADES:

I do
As well. The blood grows out like locks of hair
As red as sunset.

ORESTES:

Hanging everywhere
Are heads of those who came before us. They
Are hanging from the walls.

PYLADES:

And I would say
They are but souvenirs of sacrifice.
I say the heads are giving us advice
To keep our heads.

ORESTES:

And I believe our eyes
Must stay alert to stave off a surprise.
(He calls to Apollo:)
Apollo, once again you lead me to
A mystery. Your oracles come true
But point to new disasters. Once I held
A sword and killed my mother, though compelled
By your clear order and in name of my
Dear father who was murdered by her. I
Was then tormented by the Furies, and
Then I was banished, driven from the land
That was my birthright. Oh the long, long road
I've traveled for you, hoping signs would bode
Well and my travels would not be in vain
As I went on while suffering in pain

And far past madness. But you called to me
And said I must leave Greece and dare the sea
To bring me here to Tauric lands, where your
Great sister Artemis has temples for
Her worshipers. And there, within the shrine,
A statue in her likeness. From divine
And high Olympus it fell here, and now
You order me to rescue it. I vow
To do as you command and find a way
To steal it from this temple. And you say
I must deliver it to Athens though
You gave me no instructions. Even so,
You give me your assurance that at last
My days of pain will perish in the past.
Now I am here as you have ordered. In
A strange and hostile land. And once again,
It's Pylades beside me.
(*Addresses* PYLADES:)
                              Trusted friend,
You've shared this journey when there seems no end.
What can we do? The walls all climb so high
And stretch around all sides. So should we try
To scale them? Though could we remain unseen
If we dared try? Or should we pry between
The doors and hinges holding them? We are
Not experts in such matters and so far
From home. If they discover us, we'll be
Arrested and then executed. We
Must flee this place at once, returning to
Our ship. That is the only thing to do.

                              PYLADES:
No, we will not retreat or flee. How could
We stand to see ourselves again? And would
We dare defy the oracle? Instead,
Let's hide ourselves within the caves and head
Where water from the sea can splash them. So

We'll stay far from the ship. They will not know
We're here and tell their king. Then they may take
Us prisoner. But then by night we'll make
A swift return as darkness sheds a tear
That washes out the sunlight. We'll be here
And use all means that we can muster to
Remove the sacred statue. We'll come through
Those openings rappelling to the floor
Right there beside those columns by that door.
We're only worth what we are worth, no less.
And bravely we can face this. Second guess
Yourself? That is the coward's way, and they
Are not regarded anywhere. I say
We've come this far for something, so why turn
Around while empty-handed?

ORESTES:

I could learn

A lot from listening to you. You say
Such words of wisdom. And we must obey
The oracle for certain. So inside
The caves we go, and then we'll wait and hide.
The oracle expects our guarantee
It comes to full fruition. We must be
Young men of valor and must have no fear.
We need to face our fate. Someone is here.

(ORESTES *and* PYLADES *exit quickly as* CHORUS OF GREEK
WOMEN *enter.*)

CHORUS:

How silently I step as I walk within
How carefully I step as I walk within
These sacred holy halls
These sacred holy halls

I am torn from Greece
Torn from my home
I am a castaway

Cast out across the sea
But I am still a daughter of Greece
Yet so so far from the mountains of Greece

I dream of the mountains and the hills of Greece
Where the sea washes over the rocks and sand
And the forest grows thick and it hides the land
In my long-lost home of Greece
In the long-lost land of Greece
And my mind can reach to see it
In the memories I hold
But I cannot hold them forever
And their light is growing cold
And time moves all too swiftly
Flowing out just like a stream
The memories grow darker
Like the shadow of a dream

Though here I serve a daughter of Greece
A child of Agamemnon
The daughter of Agamemnon
She who holds the keys

In this consecrated place   I am here to serve
In these sacred holy halls   Iphigenia
In this sacred sacred space   I am here to serve
                                 a daughter of Greece

Iphigenia
The daughter of Agamemnon
The daughter of Great Agamemnon

(IPHIGENIA *re-enters.*)

IPHIGENIA:

You women are bound to me
As I am bound to this temple
Within these holy walls
My cries will sing through the halls
For in the night I saw the sight of a brother

A brother passed away
Just as the night has passed away

CHORUS:

Like the shadow of a dream
Like the shadow of a dream

IPHIGENIA:

A brother lost
A family lost
The House of Atreus lost to dust

CHORUS:

Like the shadow of a dream
Like the shadow of a dream

IPHIGENIA:

Far beyond the darkness
Far within the shadow
My brother lies in Hades

CHORUS:

Like the shadow of a dream
Like the shadow of a dream

IPHIGENIA:

And robbed the House of Atreus
Of its only son
And its only brother

So now I pour libations
Upon this sacred ground
Libations of milk and wine
Milk of the mountain cows
And the gift of the vine
The gift of Dionysus
And the honey of the bees
From their hives that fill the trees

Far away
Away in Hades
May a dead man hear my call

May a dead man hear it all
May my sacrifice bring you peace
Even only for a moment
Even for a fleeting moment

        CHORUS:

Like the shadow of a dream
Like the shadow of a dream

(IPHIGENIA *calls to the women.*)

        IPHIGENIA:

Bring forth the bowl of gold
The holy bowl of gold

(IPHIGENIA *is handed a libation bowl.*)

        IPHIGENIA:

I offer up to Hades
God of the Underworld
God of Death
Let the words upon my lips
The words upon my breath
Reach my brother
The son of Agamemnon
As I am far away
I am so far away

IPHIGENIA:	CHORUS:
So far from home	I am torn from Greece
And the happiness of home	Torn from my home
Far from the land	I am a castaway
Where my forefathers walked	Cast out across the sea
So far away	But I am still a daughter of Greece

You can't hear my tears
Though you think I am lost

        Yet so so far from

                          The mountains of Greece
And you think I am dead
But I am here
Far away   Far away
From my long-lost home
   of Greece
From my long-lost home
   of Greece

CHORUS:

We sing a song for you
Let our voices carry through
To Hades
May our song be heard in Hades
May it be heard by the dead
As we sigh for the House of Atreus
As we cry for the House of Atreus
As we mourn for the House of Atreus
For the first-born son of Atreus
We sing a song for you
Let our voices carry through
For the curse on the House of Atreus
For the generations lost to death
For the pain that leads to pain
For the web that Fate has spun
For the things we can't explain

IPHIGENIA:

From the day I was born
The beginning of my life
Fate spun a web
And wove it with strife
I was born to a mother
Who handed me unhappily
To a father who
Handed me so happily
As a sacrifice
I believed I was to be a bride

And I did not know they would hide
The truth from me
By means of a veil of lies

But now I perish
Slowly perish
Day after day after day after day
In this foreign land
This hostile land
So very far away

IPHIGENIA: CHORUS:
From my long-lost home   From her long-lost home
From my long-lost land   From her long-lost land
Of Greece Greece Greece
  Greece

Unbound by land   I am torn from Greece
Unbound by home   Torn from my home
Unbound by husband   I am a castaway
Unbound by kin   Cast out across the sea

IPHIGENIA & CHORUS:
But I am still a daughter of Greece
Yet so so far from the mountains of Greece

IPHIGENIA:
And a brother who is dead
And a brother who is dead
A brother lost
A family lost
The House of Atreus lost to dust
Like the shadow of a dream

IPHIGENIA & CHORUS:
Like the shadow of a dream
Like the shadow of a dream

LEADER OF THE CHORUS:
A herdsman comes within. What could it be
He comes to tell you?

(HERDSMAN *enters and addresses* IPHIGENIA*:*)

HERDSMAN:
I respectfully
Request a word. I fear I must report
Some most distressing news to you.

IPHIGENIA:
What sort
Of news could summon such astonishment?

HERDSMAN:
Oh, Agamemnon's daughter, I was sent
To tell you two young men have landed here.
They sailed across the sea and fought to clear
The clashing stones, and they succeeded. So
They step upon our lands. Now you must go
Prepare the ritual and offering
To Artemis. Now quickly, you must bring
The holy water and anointments.

IPHIGENIA:
How
Were they enrobed? And did their clothes allow
A hint of where they hail from?

HERDSMAN:
I could see
That they are Greek and that I guarantee.
But I know nothing further.

IPHIGENIA:
Did you hear
Their names so you can tell me?

HERDSMAN:
It was clear
That one is known as "Pylades".

IPHIGENIA:
And his
Companion?

HERDSMAN:
I'm afraid that no one is
Aware as it remains unspoken.

IPHIGENIA:
But
How did you chance to see them? Tell me what
You did to capture them?

HERDSMAN:
We all were on
The shore.

IPHIGENIA:
But why would herdsmen all be drawn
Onto the most unfriendly, rocky shore?

HERDSMAN:
To wash our herds within the sea.

IPHIGENIA:
Still, more
True confirmation is required. You
Must start again and from the start. I do
Not sacrifice men easily. Again,
How did you come to capture them? How in
The name of Zeus did they arrive here? Why
Would they both brave the wild sea and sky
And dare to travel all this way? There's no
Blood of the Greeks upon this altar, so
If it is to be drawn, there has to be
A reason they have crossed the raging sea.

HERDSMAN:
We brought our cattle to the sea that flows
In from the clashing stones. But then it goes
Into a shallow cave carved out from all
The constant waves that rise above then fall.
Some fishermen take shelter there. Just then
Another herdsman took sight of two men.
Then he retreated quietly and crept

Back to us saying, "Look, the sea has swept
Two Gods upon the shore!" And then a man
Among us who is so devout then ran
Toward the sea and called above and said,
"Oh Gods who guard the ships at sea and led
These two divine and noble beings here,
We praise you, and we raise our voice in cheer!"
But then at once another man so bold
And foolish in his heresy then told
Us all that our devotion was in vain
And said that they were shipwrecked to explain
Their presence. And he said, "They must have heard
We sacrifice all strangers here." Each word
He spoke seemed most agreeable to all
The herdsmen gathered. Then there was a call
To hunt them down in name of Artemis
And offer up their lives to her. But this
Is when the stranger, he without a name
That's known to us, then left the cave and came
Upon us. First he stood so still, but then
His head began to shake so hard. And when
He opened up his mouth, a wild groan
Came out and shook the air. And then each bone
Within his hands began to shake. He walked
Around in great confusion. Then he talked
To his companion, madder with each word,
And stalked as if he hunted down a bird
That flew around his head. And then he cried,
"Oh Pylades, they come from every side!
This serpent that is here before me, she
Has come from Hades coming after me
And means to kill me with her hundred heads
With fire breathing from each one. She shreds
My skin with claws while, tucked beneath her arm,
My mother's corpse is there and bleeding. Harm
Is here and now upon me. She will throw
Me on the jagged rocks that lie below,

And there is no escape!" We all then tried
To see what he described. And then inside
His human frame there came a sound so low
Just like a wild animal. I know
They say the Furies make such sounds. And we
Were all so frightened, standing quietly
And worried we'd be slaughtered. And just then
He drew his sword and rushed right past the men
And ran just like a lion to our cows.
And swinging wide his iron tool, he plows
Our herds by slicing them across the flank,
Believing they were Furies. And the dank
Blue sea went red with blood as many cows
Dropped dead from injury. The sight did rouse
The men to action. Many took up arms
Or blew the conch to summon men from farms
Surrounding us. Because it seemed too true
That we were both outmatched against these two
Young men that seemed accustomed to a fight,
And soon more men had gathered. But then right
That moment all the madness disappeared
Across his tear-filled eyes. The storm just cleared
Within him, though foul foam still wet his chin
Just like the sea that touched his feet. Within
A moment we attacked him, seeing he
Was out of sorts, subdued and silent. We
All took the opportunity to throw
Large stones at him and tried to strike a blow.
And each man did his part. But then there came
The other man. The stranger with a name
We know. So tenderly he wiped the face
Of his companion, firmly but with grace.
He then removed his lustrous robe, and then
He covered up his friend to shield him. When
We all prepared to strike again, he held
His friend so tight, protecting him, compelled
By something more than kindness. And by then

The stranger found his sense again. The men
Were now both ready, facing us. The one
Whose name is still unknown saw we weren't done
With our attack and made a moan so loud.
But we would not stand down. We simply plowed
Ahead and threw more stones from every side.
He looked around with dread, and then he cried
Out, "Pylades, I know that we will die,
But we will die with honor! Show the sky
Your sword and swing it down and follow me."
We saw them swing their swords and turned to flee
Into the nearby woods. But as we ran,
Some still threw stones at them, as every man
That could continued fighting them, so brave,
Attacking them in circles like a wave
Upon the sea we ran from. But it was
All done in vain, amazingly, because
With all the men we had, we could not hit
These men at all. And even knowing it
Was all in name of Artemis, we failed.
But maybe, by her grace, we then prevailed?
We formed a circle all around them and
With difficulty threw stones at each hand
That held a sword. Then when they dropped them, we
Then took them as they fell onto a knee,
So overcome from fighting. And we brought
Them both to see the King, and when he got
One look at them, he ordered us to bring
Them to the temple as an offering
And sacrifice to Artemis. I say,
Oh purest maiden, is this not a way
To finally avenge the sacrifice
Attempted on you? Let this deed suffice
To finally return the suffering
The Greeks all brought upon you. I will bring
These strangers to you. Let that foulest day
In Aulis be avenged at last I say.

LEADER OF THE CHORUS:
Your story is engaging. We must know,
Who is this madman? And why would he go
Across unfriendly seas to travel far
And seek us out?

IPHIGENIA:
I've heard enough. You are
To bring the men to me at once while I
Prepare the ritual.

(HERDSMAN *exits.*)

IPHIGENIA:
Should I now try
Retrieving what I used to have inside?
This heart I have is strange to me. I tried
Remembering the days it could contain
Compassion for a stranger. Now I strain
To shed a tear for my own countrymen.
But these two strangers won't engage me when
They are delivered here. The dreams I've seen
Within dark nights have stranded me between
The wild and the civilized, and now
I know Orestes is now dead and how
He'll never see the sun again. So should
A stranger stumble onto me, they would
Be wise to know that there is not goodwill
Within me anymore. And so until
My final day, my friends, I guarantee
That I won't feel compassion. Destiny
Has not been kind, so I in turn won't show
A hint of pity even if I know
That they have suffered more than me. But why,
If Zeus has sent a wind from Greece, do I
Not see a ship that carries Helen here
Along with Menelaus? I would cheer
As I enacted vengeance. They destroyed
My life, and I would rather be deployed

To guarantee their sacrifices. I
Would reenact that day in Aulis. My
Dark memories are still intact how men
Of Greece all overpowered me and then
Prepared to slaughter me just like a cow
With my own father demonstrating how
To slit the skin and let the blood flow. I
Had begged my father not to kill me. My
Young hand reached up to touch his beard. I said
While supplicating, "Will you see me dead?"
Upon the ground I pleaded, asking why
He would deceive me, telling me that my
Own wedding was intended for that day.
Instead, he planned to send me far away
To darkest Hades. How I pleaded to
Be bound in marriage, not be bound to do
A ceremony with a bloody end.
I knew my mother had arrived to tend
To wedding preparations, and she brought
Some Argive women with her. They did not
Arrive to see me slaughtered. No, they came
To sing the wedding hymns and praise my name
As I walked into womanhood. Instead
They found they had arrived to see me dead
And by the hand of my own father, he
Who gave me life. With every word and plea
I grew more anxious on my wedding day
With hopes he would not give my life away
To Hades. But my father's treachery
Was set in motion. I would never see
My home again, although I never said
Goodbye to anyone as I was led
To think that this was just my wedding day.
And I would never go so far away
That I would never see them both again,
My brother or my sister. I was in
The finest veil that hid my face from those

Who looked upon me. And who would suppose
The bride was only walking to her grave?
And poor Orestes, though I could not save
You from the death that stalked you, always know
That though our father failed me, you can go
Away to Hades knowing that no blame
Is on you for our father's greatest shame.
Still, let me question how the Goddess can
Insist upon refusing any man
To seek her altar if he was unclean
From killing other men or was obscene
For touching women giving birth or tried
To touch the dead, but yet they go inside
Her temple and their sacrifices are
Permitted with her pleasure. This is far
Beneath Her as the daughter of Great Zeus
And Leto. And there is no good excuse
For so much ignorance. I say until
It can be proven that the holy will
Of Artemis at last is proven true,
No murdering of trespassers. We do
Not need more bloodshed. I do not believe
The Gods approve of this. How men deceive
Themselves and others, saying that the will
Of Gods is what is telling them to kill.
If you must kill, then you must take the blame.
Don't do it in a God's most-holy name.
(She exits.)

CHORUS:

On the edge of every sea
On the sand upon each shore
There are men
You will find men
With a thirst for more
With a thirst for so much more

The sea is wide and dark
Stretching out beyond the eye
But men will try to cross it
But the men must hoist a sail
While a bird can quickly fly
Yes the men must sail
Far beyond the eye
Far beyond the sky
As the wind holds in their sail
Knowing they may fail

Men seek riches
Men seek adventure
Men will travel far
Oh so far where barbarians rule
So so far where the Gods will not follow
Men seek riches
Men seek adventure
Men will travel far
Until they don't know where they are
Men seek riches
Oh so far where barbarians rule
But only find madness
So so far where the Gods will not follow
Until they don't know where they are
Until they don't know who they are

Sailing far to foreign shores
Digging hard with oaken oars
Fighting against the will of the sea
Fighting to fill the will of the sail
Traveling far from pier to pier
Riding the sea like a charioteer
Traveling to the ends of the earth
Only concerned with what they are worth
Traveling far from here to there
But never arriving anywhere

But listen to the words of my lady's prayer
Listen to the words of our priestess here
She calls for Helen
Hopes that Helen
Will one day come here

From Troy   Men seek riches
Far away Troy   Men seek adventure
May the Gods all hear the
    prayer   Men will travel far
Iphigenia has made   Oh so far where barbarians
                          rule
And let Helen feel   So so far where
    her blade   the Gods will not follow
Let her wear a crown   Men seek riches
A crown of blood   Men seek adventure
Let her throat feel   Men will travel far until
    the blade   they don't know where
                              they are
Let a sacrifice be made   Men seek riches
                          Oh so far
For the sacrifices made   Where barbarians rule
                          But only find madness
For Helen   So so far where the Gods
For Helen   Will not follow
Helen   Until they don't know
Helen   where they are
Helen   Until they don't know
Helen   who they are

I dare to dream and pray
I pray that soon one day
That the men who seek out fame
Boldest men who cross the sea
By the Gods one day arrive here
And come to rescue me
Let brave men of Greece arrive here
From far across the sea

And may they rescue me
And may they rescue me

LEADER OF THE CHORUS:
The two young men arrive. Their hands are bound.
The herdsman's message surely now is found
To be most truthful. Silence now, my friends.
The fruit of Greece arrives, to find all ends
In sacrifice.

(LEADER OF THE CHORUS *speaks as* CHORUS *pray.*
IPHIGENIA *re-enters as* ORESTES *and* PYLADES *enter in*
shackles, brought in by GUARDS.)

LEADER OF THE CHORUS:
Oh Artemis, we pray
You find our acts acceptable. And may
Our work be worthy even though we see
This ritual as most unholy. We
Are unaccustomed to this custom.

IPHIGENIA:
And
It is but what it is. It should be planned
To please the Goddess. My priority
Is guaranteeing everything will be
As it should be.
(*To* GUARDS)
Release their hands. As they
Are made to be an offering, I say
Those bonds appear unholy. You should go
Within the temple. I am sure you know
What preparations are required there
For these esteemed occasions.

(GUARDS *exit as* IPHIGENIA *turns to* ORESTES *and*
PYLADES.)

IPHIGENIA:
Tell me where
I'll find the one who bore you. And the man

Who fathered you? And did he ever plan
An ending such as this for his fine son?
Have you a sister? Is there anyone
Who will protect her with a brother slain?
Who knows what deadly plans the Gods ordain.
We never know what darkness comes. We are
At mercy of the future. You are far
From home, unhappy strangers. Tell me where
You come so far away from. Why you dare
Set foot upon a foreign shore. Although
You now will travel to a world below
To darkness where the light will not return.

ORESTES:

How is it that you say you want to learn
About our past as presently you say
Our future has no promise? And the way
You show us pity while you still prepare
To murder us. Who are you lady? Where
Do you come from that you would think it wise
To weep and wail as tears fill up your eyes.
Will that hold back your blade? So should I wail
And hope it covers up my fear or flail
About in hope that might delay my fate
And let you find me foolish? It's too late.
A sacrifice is imminent. We know
That there is no escape. So we will show
Some dignity in death. Do not believe
We do not know what happens here. Don't grieve
The consequences of your actions.

IPHIGENIA:
Who

Is known as Pylades? Which one of you?
Just let me start with that.

ORESTES:
If you must know,

It's him. Now are you satisfied?

IPHIGENIA:
And so
You hail from Greece. Which city-state?

ORESTES:
And why
Would you need knowledge of our homeland? I
Have no idea.

IPHIGENIA:
Are you brothers?

ORESTES:
We
Are bound by more than brotherhood and see
Ourselves as more than family, but we're free
Of bonds of blood.

IPHIGENIA:
Your father, surely he
Picked out a name for you?

ORESTES:
I only know
That I am called "unfortunate".

IPHIGENIA:
Although
That is not what I asked you. Can you not
Begrudge me knowledge of your name?

ORESTES:
I've got
A name that you can't have. So when I die
You cannot mock it.

IPHIGENIA:
Can you tell me why
Your pride will not allow this?

ORESTES:
You can make

My body be your offering. But take
My name? I will not let you.

> IPHIGENIA:
> And again,

What city-state can claim you?

> ORESTES:
> I am in

No mood to educate you. What you ask
Has no true bearing on your chosen task.

> IPHIGENIA:

I ask the smallest favor. Now will you
Enlighten me?

> ORESTES:
> I come from Argos. Do

You know the famous city?

> IPHIGENIA:
> Do you swear

In name of all the Gods that it is where
You come from? Were you born there?

> ORESTES:
> Yes I was.

> IPHIGENIA:

Why did you leave then? Could it be because
Of banishment?

> ORESTES:
> I say I had to flee

By my own hand and other hands.

> IPHIGENIA:
> Tell me

Just one small thing that I must know.

> ORESTES:
> I say

What further inconvenience here today
Could be much worse than what is imminent?

                    IPHIGENIA:
I say that it is clear that you are sent
By Fate. A miracle from Argos.

                    ORESTES:
                      I
Do not believe it. But feel free to try
To if you must. Enjoy yourself.

                    IPHIGENIA:
                 I think
You know of Troy. It's infamous.

                    ORESTES:
                     The stink
Of that foul place offends me, even though
I never went there, and I only know
It from a dream. A dream I wish that I
Had never had.

                    IPHIGENIA:
             But can a city die?
They say that it is dead and gone. The spear
Of Greece has killed it.

                    ORESTES:
              Yes it would appear
That it is true, as everybody knows.

                    IPHIGENIA:
Did Helen then return? And she still shows
Her face to Menelaus?

                    ORESTES:
              It is true.
And her return was consequential to
One dear to me.

                    IPHIGENIA:
          Then where does she now dwell?

I have a right to know it. Will you tell
Me where she lies? She owes a debt to me,
One she cannot repay.

ORESTES:
I say that she
Is neither here nor there but everywhere.

IPHIGENIA:
Though I cannot imagine she would dare
Allow her shadow over Greece.

ORESTES:
I do
Know how it is entangled through and through
Within her many treacheries.

IPHIGENIA:
And is
It true the Greeks have all returned?

ORESTES:
This quiz
You give to me is thorough. Everything
Is asked of me and all at once. You bring
Me question after question.

IPHIGENIA:
But I need
To have your answers with the greatest speed.
Your time is fleeting.

ORESTES:
Question me some more.
It's very clear that you are desperate for
Some answers.

IPHIGENIA:
Was a seer with them as
They all returned from Troy? The one who has
The name of Calchas?

ORESTES:
He did not return
As he died there.

IPHIGENIA:
And I am glad to learn
That, and I praise Great Artemis. And what
About Odysseus?

ORESTES:
He's living but
He wanders near and far yet never makes
His way to home.

IPHIGENIA:
I hope his voyage takes
His life before he ever lives to see
His home again.

ORESTES:
Don't waste a curse as he
Already drowns in misery.

IPHIGENIA:
But then
How did Achilles, bravest of the men,
Come out the other side of war? Is he
Alive as well?

ORESTES:
Oh no, his destiny
Was not to live. Just like the pitied bride
Who once believed she'd kneel right at his side
Forever bound.

IPHIGENIA:
The darkest cruelest day.
Or so I've heard.

ORESTES:
From everything you say

It seems you know so much of Greece. Who can
You be?

> IPHIGENIA:
> Well, Greece is where my life began.
And where it ended.

> ORESTES:
> I can see why you
Want news of home, dear lady.

> IPHIGENIA:
> Yes I do
And mostly of a leader that they say
Now prospers.

> ORESTES:
> Who can that be? There's no way
The one I knew could be called prosperous
Or fortunate.

> IPHIGENIA:
> The son of Atreus.
The Great King Agamemnon.

> ORESTES:
> I don't know,
So do not ask me that.

> IPHIGENIA:
> I would be so
Delighted and relieved if you could say
Just one good word about him. Oh, I pray
To all the Gods at once you will.

> ORESTES:
> He's dead.
The wretched man is dead. But first he led
Another to her death.

> IPHIGENIA:
> How can it be

That he is gone? What happened to him? He
Is lost for good while I am never found?

ORESTES:

You wail so bitterly with tears unbound.
Were you related?

IPHIGENIA:

I just mourn the man

He was.

ORESTES:

And murdered by a fiendish plan

Enacted by a fiendish woman.

IPHIGENIA:

Who

Could be more wretched? Being one to do
The act or one whose blood is spilled?

ORESTES:

No more!

Ask no more questions of me.

IPHIGENIA:

I implore

You. Please at least inform me of his wife.
Is she among the living?

ORESTES:

No, her life

Was taken from her by her only son.

IPHIGENIA:

What horrors on one house! What deed was done
To make him want to kill her?

ORESTES:

It was in

Revenge upon the one who dared the sin
Of murdering his father.

IPHIGENIA:
That is why?
A murder for a murder? Should we try
To weigh which act is heavier with sin?

ORESTES:
But he has faced misfortune. He is in
The right but runs afoul of Fortune. So
The Gods do not protect him.

IPHIGENIA:
Do you know
If Agamemnon left a child in
His home?

ORESTES:
Yes, there is one that is within
The home he left: Electra. She is there
And still untouched.

IPHIGENIA:
But tell me, do I dare
Ask you about the one they killed that day
In Aulis?

ORESTES:
I just know she's far away
In darkest Hades.

IPHIGENIA:
As unhappy as
The father who destroyed her. Now he has
A home in Hades too.

ORESTES:
And all for what?
A worthless sacrifice to save a slut?

IPHIGENIA:
But what about the son who lives? Is he
In Argos?

ORESTES:
He just wanders constantly
To everywhere but never anywhere.

IPHIGENIA:
My foolish dreams were false then.

ORESTES:
Be aware
That not all dreams are true. And dare I say
That not all Gods are wise in every way,
The way that you were told. No God or dream
Can ever be exactly what they seem,
And neither can be trusted. Don't rely
On oracles or augurs. Simply try
Accepting that some inconsistency
Is possible in things we cannot see.

LEADER OF THE CHORUS:
But what of me with family so far
Away? And still we don't know if they are
Alive or dead. But tell me who could know?
They lost us all so very long ago.

IPHIGENIA:
Just listen to me. I have hatched a plan
That benefits us all. We just began
A quick acquaintance, but I think that we
Can come together in alliance. See
How quickly all our fortunes are aligned.
I have a letter here that needs to find
Its way to Argos just as you do, so
If I should spare you, stranger, would you go
And find my friends that live there? And then give
A scroll that will inform them that I live.
And one day, that a prisoner of war
Wrote this of me: He didn't blame me for
My actions, and he said it was so clear
That I am forced to do this out of fear.

He said he would not call me murderess
But just a victim under great duress.
No choice but to obey the holy will
Of Artemis. I held his scroll until
The day that I could find a way to take
The message to my home. You cannot make
A messenger of one you sacrifice,
So someone must be spared. Can I entice
You with this bargain, stranger? I can see
From how you speak and stand nobility
Runs through your blood, and surely you must know
The people I am seeking out. And so
It is so simple: Simply take the scroll
To Argos. In exchange, I can control
What happens in the temple. You will be
Rewarded with your life. But destiny
Still has ensnared your friend. As they demand
A sacrifice, I must go forth as planned.
The Goddess must be pleased, so he will be
A sacrifice, although you will go free.

ORESTES:

All that you say is well thought out, although
You have not yet considered I am so
Devoted to this man I never could
Agree, as it would kill me. I have stood
As helmsman on this darkest voyage, and
He only is a sailor, though he'll stand
Beside me with no worry for his own
Concerns. But this is mine and mine alone,
So I cannot allow it. Doing you
A favor and then save myself, but through
My freedom he is slaughtered? But you see
There is another way: You slaughter me
And send him off to Argos. It's the same
For you in any case. There is great shame
To be a man who sacrifices friends

In order to protect himself. The ends
Can never justify the means. Please see
This man is my true friend, and he must be
Allowed to live. His life is precious as
My own to me.

IPHIGENIA:
Your noble spirit has
Most clearly sprung from strongest roots. I see
A man who truly knows the way to be
The truest friend to all his friends. If there
Was one within my family who would dare
Show such devotion. Though, kind stranger, I
Still have a brother somewhere, although my
Eyes never can behold him. If you say,
This man should take your place, and you will pay
The price and be the sacrifice, as you
Could almost seem enthusiastic to
Now take his place.

ORESTES:
But who will do the deed
And sacrifice me?

IPHIGENIA:
There's no choice but heed
My sacred duty to the Goddess.

ORESTES:
Though
It is not something to be envied so
Unholy beyond words.

IPHIGENIA:
But I must do
What I must do. I have to see it through.

ORESTES:
A woman tasked with sacrificing men?
So you shall wield the blade and kill me then?

IPHIGENIA:
No, I will just prepare you for the rite,
Anointing you with holy water.

ORESTES:
                              Might
I ask you then just who the slayers are?

IPHIGENIA:
Within this holy temple, very far
Inside the walls, are men whose only task
Is sacrificing.

ORESTES:
              Do I dare to ask
What type of tomb is my new home?

IPHIGENIA:
                                  The light
Of holy flame will cleanse as we ignite
Your body in her holy name. And then
The cracks within the cave will hold you when
Your light goes dark forever.

ORESTES:
                            Pity me
If only that a sister's hand could be
The one preparing me.

IPHIGENIA:
                    Your wishes are
To be but wasted, stranger. She is far
Away for certain from this savage land.
But you are still from Greece, so from my hand
You'll find a sister's kindness. There will be
Great ornaments and ointments thoroughly
Adorning you, and then the fire will
Glow with the deepest reds as I fulfill
My duty and add sweetest honey by
The coals. Now I must go within and try
Retrieving that most-precious scroll. And please

I beg of you forgive me. All of these
Foul actions are not mine.

(IPHIGENIA *calls to* GUARDS, *who enter during the*
following:)

IPHIGENIA:
Come guards, within.
Keep watch on them, but do not put them in
Those binds again. But I'm unbound now, so
I will send word to Argos. They will know
At last I am alive. The ones I love
The most will praise Olympus up above
To know for certain that I did survive
The sacrifice and I am still alive.

(IPHIGENIA *exits.* CHORUS *begins to vocalize under the*
following:)

LEADER OF THE CHORUS:
I pity you, the one engaged to be
The one anointed. Now your destiny
Is stained with blood that soon will mingle red
With clearest holy water when you're dead.

ORESTES:
Your pity is appreciated, though
I need it not as I prepare to go.

(CHORUS *sings to* PYLADES*:*)

CHORUS:
Oh young man we honor you
As fortune shines a light
A light that guides you to your homeland
You will soon return to your homeland
On this day set on the voyage home
On this day
On this day
Fortune lights the way
Fortune lights the way

PYLADES:
But do not envy me if journey's end
Means that I need to sacrifice a friend.

CHORUS:
To turn around and head for home
If what is left behind
Could truly be what is your home
What you leave behind
Will weigh upon your mind
I do not know what I must do
Do I mourn for you or you
Do I mourn for you or you

ORESTES:
By all the Gods, my one true friend, have you
Felt something happen here that seems too true?

PYLADES:
To what are you referring? I don't know,
So I can have no answer.

ORESTES:
She is so
Just like a Greek. This woman asking me
Of Troy, the Greek's return and Calchas, he
The master of all omens, yet she seems
To know more than she should and speaks of dreams.
She mentions Great Achilles and she cries
While speaking Agamemnon's name, then tries
To seek out Clytemnestra's fate and all
The fates of her beleaguered children. Call
Me mad, but I am almost certain she
Is Greek. Or tell me why she seeks to see
A letter sent to Argos. It is clear
That she perceives the fate of Argos dear
To her and shares in our prosperity.

PYLADES:
The clues you noted did not slip past me,

And I agree except for one small thing:
It seems that all the business of a king
Is known to one and all. But I am not
Preoccupied with that as I have got
Another topic on my mind.

ORESTES:
What could
It be? If you enlighten me, it would
Perhaps come clearer to you.

PYLADES:
I would be
Ashamed to live and let the light touch me
While you lay dead forever. You and I
Have sailed together from the start, so why
Should we not die together? If I go
To Argos or my homeland, they would know
How two had left but one returned, and I
Would be accused of cowardice, and my
Good name would turn to traitor. They would say,
As gossips are so base, I ran away,
Abandoning my greatest friend. So I
Could then return to safety while you die
At hands of foul barbarians. Or worse,
They'd think I took advantage of the curse
Upon the House of Atreus to see
That first I slay you, then I come to be
The King of Argos with your sister as
My wife. It would be logical. This has
No other outcome, so it seems that I
Must breathe my final breath with you and die
Together. They will slaughter us and burn
Us both as brothers, never to return
To light and life, but I will be a friend
And live with honor to the very end.

ORESTES:
Don't say such things. My grief is mine to bear,

And I will carry it and never share
It with you and compound it. What you said
About your reputation I would dread
If it were said of me as well. Could I
Cause you who have supported me to die?
I have been marked by all the Gods to be
Their plaything and a pawn. So as for me,
Swift death will be relief for certain. You
Can still have great prosperity and do
Great things within a house so pure while I
Am carrying the sinful streak of my
Accursed house. If you are spared to be
The father of my sister's children, we
Will then assure the family line will live.
The House of Atreus will prosper. Give
Your life to this endeavor. You'll command
Within my father's halls. And by my hand,
I charge you by a task that you must do
When you return to Greece and Argos: You
Will make a tomb for me, and you will set
Memorials upon it. You will get
Electra to remove a lock of hair
And leave it there along with tears. Then share
The tale with her of how a woman who
Has also hailed from Greece had led me to
My final moment, surely purified
By her fine hand right at the altar's side.
I only ask you never dare betray
Her as you see when people dare to stray
From marriage vows. It only tears apart
The house and those within it. I must start
To bid farewell, my faithful friend. How you
Have always been there for me through and through.
A fellow huntsman at my side from days
Of boyhood to my death. How many ways
Have you been burdened by my miseries?
As Great Apollo through his prophecies

Deceived me and misled me. Should we say
He drove me far from Greece to cast away
The one who proved his oracles untrue?
I gave him all my trust and faith, but through
My blind obedience I went and killed
My mother. But an oracle fulfilled
Destroyed my life as well.

PYLADES:
I swear to you
That you will have a tomb. I will stay true
To marriage and the marriage bed. I see
A friend unhappy in his life will be
Unhappy in his death as well but still
More dear to me in death. Yet wait until
The will of Great Apollo is revealed.
It's possible your fate is not yet sealed.
He may come through for you, though you may be
So close to death. His holy prophecy
Has never shown an endgame yet. Your fate
Just might reverse before it is too late.

ORESTES:
All words from you and Great Apollo fall
Far short of what is needed now. And all
Is lost. She has returned.

(IPHIGENIA *re-enters and addresses* GUARDS.)

IPHIGENIA:
Now go within.
Assist the preparations to begin
The ritual.

(GUARDS *exit. She addresses* PYLADES:)

IPHIGENIA:
This is the scroll you must
Deliver. But I wonder, can I trust
That it will find its way to Argos? I
Am worried, once released, that you will fly

As free as birds do and you will not care
About the pact we made. I am aware
That men when trapped in fear will swear and vow
But once released will soon forget. So now
I need assurance that my message will
Remain your first priority until
It reaches Argos. So how can I know?

ORESTES:
Just tell him what you want. How should he show
His true commitment putting you at ease?

IPHIGENIA:
Let him now swear an oath and prove that he's
Devoted to this task and he will see
It reaches Argos and my friends.

ORESTES:
Will we
Then be assured you keep the bargain too?

IPHIGENIA:
Just tell me what I need to say to you.

ORESTES:
You must assure that he will be set free
From these barbarians and he will be
Allowed to leave alive.

IPHIGENIA:
Of course he will.
How could he do this favor if they kill
Him?

ORESTES:
But there is a King who must allow
It.

IPHIGENIA:
I will see he's safe. You have my vow.
I will persuade the King, and I will see
Him to the ship myself.

ORESTES: *(To* PYLADES*)*
Now swear.

(To IPHIGENIA*)*

As he
Will swear devoutly, so should you.

IPHIGENIA:
So swear
You will deliver this to Greece. Once there,
You will assure it goes into the hands
Of my good friends.

PYLADES:
I leave these foreign lands
And I will go to Greece, I swear, and I
Will see your friends receive this message.

IPHIGENIA:
By
My hand you will go safely past the shore
And to your ship.

PYLADES:
Which of the Gods is your
True witness to these words?

IPHIGENIA:
Great Artemis.
I am her priestess.

PYLADES:
And I swear to this
In name of Zeus, the ruler of the sky.

IPHIGENIA:
And should you break this oath or should you try
To wrong me?

PYLADES:
Then I say I will not make
My way to home again. Should you forsake
Your vow to me?

IPHIGENIA:
Then may I never find
My way to Argos while I live.

PYLADES:
My mind
Has just considered something.

IPHIGENIA:
You must say
It now if it is vital.

PYLADES:
On my way
To Argos, what if something happens to
The ship? And then the scroll is lost? And through
The act of rescuing myself I live
But can't do what I vowed. Would you forgive
My oath?

IPHIGENIA:
Well then it seems I need to say
What is within. To find another way
To send my message would be prudent. So,
In case the scroll is lost, you still will know
All that must be communicated. And
If it is lost and you are saved, we planned
For it, and all will not be lost at sea.

PYLADES:
Your words are fine and spoken perfectly,
So worthy of the Gods and of us all.
And when I get to Argos I will call
On all your friends, but first, please tell me who
It is that I must bring this scroll from you?

IPHIGENIA:
You must seek out Orestes. Find the son
Of Agamemnon. Let him know the one
That he believes was lost in Aulis is

Alive and well. Yes, let him know that his
Long-lost Iphigenia sends this scroll.

ORESTES:
But where is she? Please tell me. Did her soul
Return from Hades?

IPHIGENIA:
She is standing here,
The one that you are speaking to. My ear
Is ringing now with all your words, and I
Cannot sort out my thoughts!
(She reads her message.)
I beg you try,
My only brother, come and rescue me.
Return me to our home in Argos. Free
Me from these foul barbarians and my
Indentures to the Goddess. Many die
From my sad hands as I am forced to make
A sacrifice of any stranger.

ORESTES:
Wake
Me now, my faithful Pylades! Where are
We?

IPHIGENIA:
It's a blight on you if I stay far
Away, Orestes. So you hear again
My brother's name. Now you must hold it in
Your memory.

PYLADES:
By all the Gods!

IPHIGENIA:
Why do
You dare invoke the Gods? Who said that you
May meddle in my business?

PYLADES:
         There is no
True reason. Please continue. I just go
Away within my thoughts to other things.
If I ask questions of you and it brings
Me answers, I may not believe them.

IPHIGENIA:
           Let
Him know how Artemis came down and set
A deer upon the altar on that day
In Aulis. So our father's sword did slay
An innocent, although it was not me.
Then I was whisked here far across the sea.
That is the information here within
The scroll.

PYLADES:
     Then I must say you locked me in
The easiest of oaths. So right away,
I will deliver it just as you say.
So here, Orestes: It's a scroll for you,
And it comes from your sister.

ORESTES:
          And I do
Receive it. But I leave it closed as I
Am overcome. No words could speak to my
Astonishment and joy. My sister, please,
Fall here in my embrace right into these
Two arms that held such doubt but only seek
To hold these wonders you reveal.

LEADER OF THE CHORUS:
         You speak
Of things beyond your reach, bold stranger. You
Are in the presence of a priestess. Do
Not dare to touch her or her garments.

ORESTES:

I
Greet you, my dearest sister sired by
Great Agamemnon. I beg you, don't turn
Your face away from me as you now learn
Your brother you thought lost is here and near
To you.

IPHIGENIA:

If you are him, why are you here?
His name rings out in Argos! Stop your lies!

ORESTES:
You are unhappy when you should be wise.
He is not found in Argos.

IPHIGENIA:

Then tell me,
Did Clytemnestra spawn you?

ORESTES:

Yes. And he
Whose grandfather was Pelops was the man
Who was my father.

IPHIGENIA:

I suppose you plan
On proving this to me.

ORESTES:

I do. Ask me
About the house of all our fathers.

IPHIGENIA:

Be
The one to start. Enlighten me.

ORESTES:

I then
Will speak Electra's words to you. Of when
Both Atreus and Thyestes engaged
In battle. Do you know of it?

IPHIGENIA:
                         They raged
A long and bloody battle I am told,
A quarrel for a ram made out of gold.

ORESTES:
Do you remember weaving such a ram
Within a detailed web?

IPHIGENIA:
                         And now I am
Beginning to believe you, and I dare
To turn my heart to you.

ORESTES:
                         And glowing there
Within the middle of the loom, the sun.
Do you remember as I do?

IPHIGENIA:
                         I spun
That shape as well within the web.

ORESTES:
                                   And were
You gifted with a bath? Did it occur
The day before you set for Aulis?

IPHIGENIA:
                         Yes,
I was to be a bride. But then distress
Was all I found that day.

ORESTES:
                         And then you gave
To Clytemnestra your fine hair to save?

IPHIGENIA:
It was for my memorial. As I
Could not give her my body

ORESTES:
                         As for my

Own recollections: I will speak to you
To prove myself. Within the walls and through
The halls of home are chambers where you slept.
And that is where an ancient spear is kept,
The one that Pelops brandished on the day
That Oenomaus fell. It's on display.

IPHIGENIA:

Oh my dearest one
I will raise my voice
May the Gods hear me
Oh oh Orestes

You the long-lost son
So far from your home
But you are near me
Oh oh Orestes

ORESTES:

And all this time I thought that you were gone,
Yet here you are alive. And there upon
Your eyes and cheeks are tears as mine have too.
Who ever thought I'd reunite with you?

IPHIGENIA:

Was it yesterday I left you
Just a baby in a nurse's arms
The youngest in the house of our fathers
Yesterday
So far away
But today is far from over
A joyous day to celebrate
You are here it is far beyond wonder
Here today
Here today

ORESTES:

From here on out may we two always be
Entwined within a happy destiny.

(IPHIGENIA *addresses* CHORUS.)

IPHIGENIA:

Raise your voices dearest companions
Raise each voice
Sing my joy
To the sky
But I fear the joy is fleeting
Winds can change and make things fly

CHORUS:

Oh oh Orestes
Oh oh Orestes

IPHIGENIA:

WInds blow from our home in Argos
Brought him here
And he is now a man
Winds of change can make everything forgotten

CHORUS:

Yesterday
Yesterday

IPHIGENIA:

Though some things are never forgotten

CHORUS:

Yesterday
Is today

IPHIGENIA:

And here I see a light before me
A son of Atreus
A son of Greece

CHORUS:

He's the son of a son of a son of Greece

IPHIGENIA:

I praise the Gods
For this son of Atreus
And may we two find peace
May we two find peace

ORESTES:
We two were born to royalty, although
The highest birth can make one fall so low.

IPHIGENIA:
Yesterday
Is so far away
Yet I still remember how my father held the blade
Yet I still remember the invocation was made
And he held the blade to my throat
As if I were a goat
As if I were a goat

ORESTES:
I feel your horror, though I was not there.
The pain I feel for you is hard to bear.

IPHIGENIA:
Bathed and primed to be a bride
And headed to the bed of Achilles
But bathed and primed
And then on my knees
Beside an altar they prepared
To find out that I was prepared
Not to lay on a marriage bed
But prepared
To be dead
From a wedding veil to a wretched wail
Preparing to be dead

CHORUS:
Yesterday
Yesterday
Yesterday

IPHIGENIA:
He cleansed me with lustral holy water
Only to sacrifice a daughter

IPHIGENIA & CHORUS:

Yesterday
Yesterday

ORESTES:

I am ashamed to know that he could be
So cold and kill his daughter callously.

IPHIGENIA:

Do not call a man a father
Who could hold an unholy blade
I am now without a father
I was remade
By the blade
Made to face calamity
Made to fight a destiny

ORESTES:

But Fate just intervened and I am spared
The ritual that you have just prepared.
And dearest sister, think how it would be
Had you found out the one you killed was me.

IPHIGENIA:

Oh my unholy hand
The dreadful thing that I had planned
For the child of Agamemnon
But now you are free from the binds of hate
Now you may escape your fate
Perhaps today is not too late
For the child of Agamemnon
You came here from a foreign land
And almost destroyed by my unholy hand
For a sacrifice by my own hand
By a child of Agamemnon

But far beyond this endless night
Might there be an end in sight
Will Fate and Fortune end their fight
Will all the Gods hold back their spite

For the children of Agamemnon
For the children of Agamemnon

Let us fly
Let us flee
Far from this city
To our destiny
What is the way to Argos
What is the path to Argos
And which way will get us through
Before the blade finds you
Before the blade finds you

Somewhere deep within
I must find the strength
Somewhere deep within
I must find the way
How you must flee
By the land or the sea
If by land you will search hard for a road
For road that was never there
Passing through uncharted lands
Right into barbarian hands
And at their hands you will find your death
In their lands you will draw your final breath

Or do you go by sea
Go sailing on your ship
Daring to tame the wild sea
And if you cross it you will be
At the clashing stones
Will you dare the clashing stones

Or will you pity me
The child of Agamemnon
Will someone help to free
The children of Agamemnon
To all the Gods I pray
Please show the one true way

If any mortal can
Give us the one true plan
When there seems no hope at all
To anyone we call
Give us your pity
Show us to peace
When all is impossible show us release
From the bonds that bind
Those who are maligned
The children of Agamemnon
The children of Agamemnon

LEADER OF THE CHORUS:
The sight I see is far beyond a tale
They tell within a fable. And words fail
Me now and will assuredly if I
Describe it in the future. This is why
To see a wondrous sight oneself is more
Engaging than to hear a tale of yore.

PYLADES:
When two who have been parted reunite
It's understandable that at first sight
Of one another after time has passed
Embracing is expected. But how fast
Our fortunes can reverse. So we must try
A quick escape, Orestes. We must fly
Beyond the borders of this foreign land
And get to safety. You must understand
The wisest men know opportunity
Is fleeting. And there is no guarantee
That Fate will favor us forever.

ORESTES:
You
Speak well my friend. But you must think this through.
If we believe our worth, then we will show
The Gods we are most worthy. And I know

Their power is far greater than what we
Possess to modify our destiny.

IPHIGENIA:
But I will not be silent. You must tell
Me of our dear Electra. Is she well?
Or merely just surviving? Just as you,
She is my first concern.

ORESTES:
She's married to
The man you see before you happily.

IPHIGENIA:
And who is this man's father? Where does he
Hail from?

ORESTES:
He is from Phocis and he is
The son of Strophius.

IPHIGENIA:
That means that his
Ancestors are of Atreus?

ORESTES:
Yes, he
Is kinsman to us by his mother. We
Are close as friends can be and one I give
My trust to.

IPHIGENIA:
I believe he did not live
When I was sacrificed in Aulis.

ORESTES:
No,
His father's house was childless for so
Long.

IPHIGENIA:
Hail to you, my sister's husband.

ORESTES:
                              Do
Salute him as my great protector too.
He is far more than a relation.

IPHIGENIA:
                         Though
You must tell me what evil drove you so
Beyond the pale that you would dare commit
The darkest act against our mother?

ORESTES:
                                It
Is something that should not be said. Just know
That I avenged our father.

IPHIGENIA:
                       What was so
Egregious that she murdered him?

ORESTES:
                          I say
It is far better you don't know the way
She came to that conclusion.

IPHIGENIA:
                     Then I will
Not ask again. But do you now fulfill
Your destiny as leader of all men
In Argos?

ORESTES:
               Menelaus took it when
They banished me beyond the borders.

IPHIGENIA:
                                 He
Then took advantage of your misery?

ORESTES:
It was the Furies. They all drove me far
Away. It was not Menelaus.

IPHIGENIA:
                        Are
You still afflicted by them? I was told
Your ravings were a horror to behold
Upon the shore today.

ORESTES:
                   And it was not
The first time I was frantic.

IPHIGENIA:
                    They have brought
These horrors onto you for killing she
Who gave you life.

ORESTES:
                 They put a bit on me
As if I were a horse and drove me to
The farthest edge of madness.

IPHIGENIA:
                      Why did you
Come here, so very far away?

ORESTES:
                     I came
By order of an oracle in name
Of Great Apollo.

IPHIGENIA:
               For what purpose? Why?
Please tell me, or are you forbidden?

ORESTES:
                            I
Will tell you how I started down this path
To infamy and to the God's great wrath.
I once was burdened with our mother's fate—
Of which I will not speak. To consecrate
And cleanse her of her sins, I did a deed
As ordered by an oracle to heed

Some dark instructions. Once the deed was done
The Furies came upon me. Though I'd run
Away from them in terror, they would be
Upon me in a moment, violently
Attacking with their screams. Then I was sent
By Great Apollo off to Athens, meant
To stand on trial with a jury drawn
From those we will not name. I came upon
The holy court in Athens. It was built
By Zeus himself when Ares held the guilt
Of murder on his blood-polluted hands.
But everywhere I faced great reprimands
And I was a pariah. I was stained
By blood and by the Gods. Though I remained
Unwelcome, some shared hospitality
But gave accommodation separately
From others, shunning me with silence. Though
They offered me an equal portion so
Like theirs but still while isolated. I
Could not condemn them, but I sat in my
Sad isolation acting as if though
Their treatment of me did not matter. So
I breathed in deeply then exhaled and seemed
So unaware I killed her. I redeemed
Myself, I hear, as they now celebrate
My misery in Athens with a great
Religious festival each year. They raise
A cup of wine up to the Gods and praise
My great misfortune. I went up the hill
Of Ares for my trial. I sat still
But there before me was a Fury. She
Then took a seat as well, opposing me.
So each side spoke their argument about
The murder of a mother. But all doubt
Was then released as Great Apollo came
And testified on my behalf. The same
Votes were against me as were for me. Tied

But free to go, though once I went outside,
Some of the Furies would not let me be.
They felt unsatisfied and came for me,
So I continued, bound in torment by
Their piercing screams. And so, tormented, I
Ran off in horror, making for the shrine
Of Great Apollo. While refusing wine
Or food of any kind, I fell and prayed
That I would find relief in death and made
A plea to he whose oracle first set
Me on a path to my destruction. "Let
Me die," I said, but then another voice
Came flooding through the shrine: "You have a choice,
Orestes. If you truly seek to be
Free from the Furies, do this task for me:
Seek out the holy statue and retrieve
It for me from a foreign land then leave
It in the Temple of Athena. You
And you alone can help me see this through."
We need the statue of the Goddess so
I can be freed from madness. Then we go
Away from here. Yes, we shall sail so fast
Upon my ship with many oars. At last
You once again will be in Greece and in
The house of all our fathers once again.
I beg of you, please give this gift to me
So we can both be free of misery.

LEADER OF THE CHORUS:

The House of Atreus is blighted by
The God's great wrath. Though they may dare to try
Escaping, how it seems to simmer on.
And it can seem their curse is never gone.

IPHIGENIA:

I dared to dream for years that once again
I'd see your face, dear brother, and within
The walls of Argos. Now I seek to share

Your dream of liberation from the snare
Of torment and to once again restore
The House of Atreus to glory, for
I hold no anger at the man who sought
To slay me. Now I'll see that you are not
A sacrifice. Then we can seek to save
Our noble home and name. But are we brave
Enough to dare concealing what we do
From Artemis and then the King? As through
Our act the pedestal will still be there.
But everyone will see that it is bare.
Then death will surely come upon me. Should
I argue my way out of peril? Would
I chance to be successful, could you take
The statue on your ship and also make
A passenger of me? A noble deed
For certain. And you would be guaranteed
A prosperous return to Argos. Though
If you should fail and I should die, you go
Away in freedom anyway. I say
That it is worth the risk, as either way
You will be saved, and that is worth far more
To me than my own life. I know that for
Our royal line to prosper, it must be
The son who will survive. My destiny
Cannot compare.

ORESTES:

I am already stained
With my own mother's blood. What could be gained
By causing you to die as well? I strive
To see we share a stake to stay alive,
Just as you do. But live or die, I'll see
You safely home. Or should your destiny
Restrain you here, then I shall too remain.
But if you think that danger lurks, explain
To me why Artemis would not agree

That we retrieve her statue? As you see,
Apollo was most clear in his command
That I retrieve it from this foreign land.
And then I find you here? Now everything
Makes sense to me. And I am here to bring
You home as well.

IPHIGENIA:
Then we must seek to see
That neither of us dies. So how can we
Achieve our goals? As home is just in view,
Yet far away.

ORESTES:
Well then, I say to you
That we could kill the King.

IPHIGENIA:
How readily
That you suggest it. Could we dare to be
A foreign guest that kills their host?

ORESTES:
Although
If it would save us, we should dare it.

IPHIGENIA:
No.
Though I appreciate your industry.

ORESTES:
But what if you were to sequester me
Within the temple?

IPHIGENIA:
Using darkness to
Conceal you, then escape?

ORESTES:
Escaping through
The night just like a thief. We'll save the day

For those who need the light to shine the way
To truth and honesty.

IPHIGENIA:
But there within
Are honor guards, and they will see you in
There.

ORESTES:
So there is no hope? How can we be
Saved?

IPHIGENIA:
With a way that just came clear to me.

ORESTES:
What is your plan? Please let me know.

IPHIGENIA:
I can
Just use your screams as cover.

ORESTES:
How you plan
With cunning skill just like all women do.

IPHIGENIA:
And I will tell them after you were through
With slaying your own mother, you arrived
From Argos.

ORESTES:
If success can be derived
From my foul suffering, then use it.

IPHIGENIA:
I
Will say you are unclean, and that is why
You cannot be a sacrifice to her.

ORESTES:
And for what reason? Though I feel so sure
I know the answer.

IPHIGENIA:
I will make it clear
That you are most unclean, and they will fear
To give what is unholy to her.

ORESTES:
How
Can we retrieve the statue?

IPHIGENIA:
I will vow
To them that I will purify you in
The waves upon the sea.

ORESTES:
Yet still within
The temple walls, the statue we came to
Retrieve is still beyond our grasp.

IPHIGENIA:
And you
Have touched it, so I'll say how it is now
Unclean and must be cleansed as well.

ORESTES:
And how?
Within the waves upon the sea as well?

IPHIGENIA:
Down where your ship rides on the ocean's swell
While held at anchor.

ORESTES:
But who will it be
Who bears the statue, bringing it to me?

IPHIGENIA:
It only can be me. No other hand
May touch the holy image.

ORESTES:
Have you planned
How Pylades will figure in our plot?

IPHIGENIA:
I will announce his hands are also fraught
With blood and most-unholy murder.

ORESTES:
                                    So
The King, quite unaware, will never know
What you are doing?

IPHIGENIA:
                        I will frame our plot
With sweet convincing words as there is not
Another way that we can hide.

ORESTES:
                                And my
Great ship with many oars is ready.

IPHIGENIA:
                                    I
Then trust in you to see that safely we
Escape.

ORESTES:
            Yet there is one thing left to see:
How can we know these women present here
Will not reveal our plans? Go fill their ear
With most convincing words. A woman has
Great strength, inspiring great pity as
She utilizes truth. As for the rest,
You can rely on me.

(IPHIGENIA *addresses* CHORUS.)

IPHIGENIA:
                    I must request,
My truest friends, to let me be in your
Protection, should I be triumphant or
If I should fail and never get to see
The shores of Greece again and live to be
With my dear brother and my sister. Then

Let my words now remind you all that when
You are a woman, you are circled by
A bond with other women, so we try
Protecting other women when we find
Our common needs are often intertwined.
I ask you all for silence and to see
That we escape these walls successfully.
All words have weight, and you must hold them when
You hold a confidence. Now these two men
And I are now entwined within one fate,
And through the ties of blood and love, we wait
To see if we return to our own land
Or languish here and die. Please understand,
If I am safe, then I will see that you
Are all returned to Greece as well. Now, through
An oath to seal this pact, I ask you all
To raise your right hand high as I now call
Upon your memories of home. Now you
And you and you and all of you. Break through
Your cage of staid compliance here. Think of
Your mother and your father and the love
Of your lost children. Who will speak the vow?
And who might dare refuse and so allow
My brother and my kin and me to die?

Leader of the Chorus:

Do not have fear, our mistress. You must try
To see yourself as saved, as I will stay
As silent as can be just in the way
You stated. Let Great Zeus now hear my vow.

Iphigenia:

So let your words now bless you and allow
For great prosperity.
(To Orestes *and* Pylades*:)*
It now is you
Who must succeed. You now must step into
The temple as the King will soon arrive,

And he will question if you are alive
Or dead. He will demand at once I slay
You if you still draw breath.

(ORESTES *and* PYLADES *exit.* IPHIGENIA *prays:*)

IPHIGENIA:
And now I pray
To you, Great Artemis. You saved me from
My father's slaying hand, so now I come
To you again to save me and these two
I thought were strangers. If you see us through
This, all Apollo's prophecies will be
Found accurate, and mortals all will see
He is to be exalted. You should take
Your leave of these barbarians and make
Your way to Athens with your statue. You
Are far above this filth. Please see us through
Our grand escape and take us to a place
Where everyone is worthy of your grace.
(*She exits.*)

CHORUS:

There is a bird
A bird that sings
Where the cliffs are high
Above the sea
Where they cut the sky
Above the sea
And the cliffs are sharp
Like the songs of the bird
And the bird's sad words
Are only heard
By a few who walk on land
By the few who understand

I am a bird
Who can barely sing
I am a bird

Who will never fly
Over the rocks
Where the cliffs rise high
Like a prison wall
Climbing by the sea
The endless sea before me
That tells me I will never see home
Oh I could sing
Of a land far away
Oh I could sing
And raise my voice
To Artemis
Artemis Artemis
And call her name
Like the way I did at home
Praying to her
By the palm trees and laurel
Calling to her
By the vine-ripened olive
Singing to her
Like a ripple on water
Like the singing of a swan
Singing as if a muse was near
Wishing that I would fly from here

And beyond the sea
There flows a river
Like the river of tears that warms my cheek
Tears that stain my cheek
I remember the spears that touched my cheek
On the day that my city fell
On the day that my city burned
On the day I was taken away
And never was returned
Barbarians brought me here
Here where I was sold
For a little bag of gold

And now I serve Agamemnon's daughter
The priestess of this temple
The priestess of Artemis
I serve by the altar
Where blood is spilled
Not the blood of a sheep
Or the blood of a lamb
Yet blood is spilled
Blood is spilled

I envy those
Who only know pain
I envy those
Who have only known pain
When you are raised to always be
A slave to harsh necessity
If you are raised in misery
And you only have known pain
Then you never will know pain
But if a happy life is marred
By misery you will be scarred
If you are not born in pain
You cannot live in pain

But you our lady
You our priestess
You will flee
You will fly
And find yourself
Once again
In Greece Greece Greece Greece
Let the music of the Gods
Drive the men who pull the oars
So again you see the shores
Of Greece Greece Greece Greece
With every stroke of the oar
Your ship goes farther from shore

As you head for a faraway pier
I remain trapped back here

I am a bird	May I fly beyond this place
Who can barely sing	May I fly across the sea
I am a bird	May I follow Apollo
Who will never fly	As he takes the sun
Over the rocks	Far across the sea

Where the cliffs rise high
Like a prison wall
Climbing by the sea
The endless sea before me
That tells me I will never see home

Oh I could sing   May the sheerest veil
Of a land far away   Cover my hair
Oh I could sing   May I be married
And raise my voice   Where I once was a maiden
To Artemis   Back in Greece
Artemis Artemis   Back in Greece
And call her name
Like the way I did at home
Praying to her   May I dance about
By the palm trees and
   laurel
Calling to her   Like the girl that I once was
By the vine-ripened olive
Singing to her   Back in Greece
Like a ripple on water   Back in Greece

Like the singing of a swan
Singing as if a muse was near
Wishing that I would fly from here
Wishing that I would fly from here

(THOAS *enters with his* GUARDS.)

THOAS:
Where can I find the Greece-born Priestess? She
Whose hand controls the temple gates. Are we

Arriving now to see the sacred rite
Is underway? And does the firelight
Surround them both in cleansing flame within
The sacred temple walls?

LEADER OF THE CHORUS:
She now walks in,
My King, to greet you. She will tell you all.

(IPHIGENIA *re-enters with the statue of Artemis.*)

THOAS:
But what is this? You leave the sacred hall
And there within your arms a statue? This
Most-holy image of Great Artemis
That never is to be removed. Tell me
Now, Agamemnon's daughter, why I see
This blasphemy.

IPHIGENIA:
My King, please step away.
Stay back within the entrance.

THOAS:
You must say
What strange occurrence causes this command.

IPHIGENIA:
My Lord and King, you need to understand
My words are quick and curt as means to clean
This holy place of sin.

THOAS:
What do you mean?
Speak clearly now.

IPHIGENIA:
The victims that were sent
To me were most unclean.

THOAS:
Did I consent

For you to have your own opinions, or
Were you informed of this?

> IPHIGENIA:
> Could I ignore

The statue turning on its own?

> THOAS:
> Was there

An earthquake? Or did it just turn?

> IPHIGENIA:
> I dare

Say it just turned by its own will, and then
It closed its eyes.

> THOAS:
> But did this happen when

The foreigners appeared? Are they unclean?

> IPHIGENIA:

They both committed acts that are obscene.
That sadly is the cause.

> THOAS:
> They dared to slay

My loyal men upon the beach today
And killed without repentance. Is that why?

> IPHIGENIA:

They came with stains of blood from home.

> THOAS:
> Now I

Must know the details of the murder.

> IPHIGENIA:
> They

Conspired with their swords to do away
With their own mother.

> THOAS:
> Great Apollo! How

Could even foul barbarians allow
A heinous act as this?

IPHIGENIA:
And that is why
They both were banished far and forced to fly.

THOAS:
And is it due to them that you now take
The holy image out?

IPHIGENIA:
I hope to make
It clean again beneath Olympus. To
Remove the stench of blood.

THOAS:
But how did you
Discover they were so polluted?

IPHIGENIA:
I
First saw the statue move and wondered why,
And I surmised it was the strangers, so
I then interrogated them.

THOAS:
I know
Your Grecian ways prepared you well, and you
Are sharper than a sword.

IPHIGENIA:
And yet they do
Me one small kindness that enraptures me.

THOAS:
They brought you news from far across the sea
In Greece?

IPHIGENIA:
They say Orestes prospers there.
He is my only brother.

THOAS:
Be aware
That news could be but bait in hopes that you,
By feeling joyful, might just save them through
A sentimental moment.

IPHIGENIA:
Then they said
My father lives and thrives.

THOAS:
Yet you were led
Back to the Goddess, tending to her as
You are devoted.

IPHIGENIA:
When a person has
A hatred that was born of being made
A sacrifice for Greece, it does not fade.

THOAS:
But still, what should we do with these two men?
Please tell me the procedure.

IPHIGENIA:
I say when
There is a question, holy law will show
The only way we should proceed.

THOAS:
Although
You have the holy water ready, and
A sharpened sword is almost in your hand.

IPHIGENIA:
But first they must be truly purified.

THOAS:
In water from the sea or springs?

IPHIGENIA:
Outside

This temple in the endless sea, a man
Can be released of foulest sin.

                        THOAS:
                    They can.
So make them worthy of the Goddess.

                        IPHIGENIA:
                            And
It will then guarantee that what I planned
Will be successful.

                        THOAS:
                    But outside the door
The waves crash close to here.

                        IPHIGENIA:
                        But we need more
Seclusion than the open air outside
Allows.

                        THOAS:
            Then you must steal away and hide
And do what you must do away from me.
I know there are some rites I should not see.

                        IPHIGENIA:
And I must bring this holy image to
Be purified as well.

                        THOAS:
                    And it seems true
That blood of matricide has fouled it.

                        IPHIGENIA:
                            Or
I never would have dared remove it for
Another purpose.

                        THOAS:
                    And I say that you
Are most devout and wise.

                    IPHIGENIA:
                    But can you do
What is required?

                    THOAS:
                    If you first will tell
Me.

                    IPHIGENIA:
    You must shackle both of them.

                    THOAS:
                            That's well
And good. But could they both escape?

                    IPHIGENIA:
                            You would
Trust men from Greece with freedom?

                    THOAS:
                            Understood.
(To GUARDS*:)*
Go get the chains.

                    IPHIGENIA:
            And see if they will bring
The strangers here.

                    THOAS:
            It shall be done.

                    IPHIGENIA:
                        And sling
Their heads within their robes.

                    THOAS:
                        So that the sun
Will not light them with holy rays?

                    IPHIGENIA:
                        May one
Or two of your attendants follow me?

THOAS:
These two can go with you.

IPHIGENIA:
Can someone see
That word gets to the city?

THOAS:
And to say?

IPHIGENIA:
That all remain within their homes.

THOAS:
Or they
May be polluted with foul homicide.

IPHIGENIA:
Some things should not be spoken of.

THOAS:
(To another GUARD:)
Go ride
Into the city warn them all.

IPHIGENIA:
Let no
Man come within the sight of us.

THOAS:
You show
Such care for your adopted city.

IPHIGENIA:
I
Owe them my loyalty.

THOAS:
I think you try
To say that you are loyal to me.

IPHIGENIA:
That
Could be correct.

THOAS:
The city holds you at
The height of their respect.

IPHIGENIA:
But can you stay

Here at the shrine?

THOAS:
For what?

IPHIGENIA:
To kneel and pray
While purifying it with firelight.

THOAS:
So you return to find it cleansed.

IPHIGENIA:
And right
As both the strangers come outside.

THOAS:
What should

I do?

IPHIGENIA:
Pull up your robe just like a hood
To cover up your eyes.

THOAS:
So I won't be
Befouled by their pollution?

IPHIGENIA:
Patiently,
You must wait here if I am gone too long.

THOAS:
But how long should you be?

IPHIGENIA:
It would be wrong
To worry.

THOAS:
You are right. Go do the task
The Goddess has commanded. Let her ask
What time may be required.

IPHIGENIA:
Let there be
A great purification righteously
Performed.

THOAS:
And I will pray beside you.

(THOAS *kneels down as a procession enters with* ORESTES
and PYLADES *in chains with their heads covered by robes
accompanied by* GUARDS. ATTENDANTS *carry wreathes, lit
torches and containers of holy water.*)

IPHIGENIA:
I
Now see the strangers are arriving by
The temple entrance. And I also see
That preparations have been made, and we
Will have some newborn lambs for sacrifice
Because their slaughter only can suffice
For cleansing men of blood with blood. Now bring
The glowing torches over here and string
The garlands with Bay Laurel. Purify
This temple and these strangers. Sanctify
Them all before the Goddess. And I call
Unto the city dwellers: Now you all
Must stay back far away from these foul men
Who reek of blood pollution. Know that when
You touch them you will be impure, and so
If you are here to cleanse your hands or go
Up to the altar seeking marriage or
Are heavy with a child, just ignore
The sight of them or you will be unclean.
Oh Artemis Great Huntress, how we mean

To honor you by stripping them of their
Foul maddening pollution. With great care,
We dare to sacrifice them in your name
And mean to purify them by the flame
Within your sacred temple. And then through
Our work we keep your temple pure as you,
If we should be so fortunate. I dare
Not speak the rest. Instead I will prepare
The ritual while all the Gods observe
Our actions, and I hope we will deserve
Your blessings, oh Great Artemis, while you
Now bless us as your holy light shines through.

(IPHIGENIA *exits with procession of* ATTENDANTS *and*
THOAS *exits into the temple with* GUARDS.*)*

CHORUS:

Oh Apollo
Great Apollo
God of the Sun and Prophecy
The golden god
Like the golden Sun
Giving light so that mortals can see
Giving light from each prophecy
Giving light so that mortals can see
What will come to be

There was a serpent who guarded all knowledge
A serpent who guarded each prophecy
You slew him Apollo
You killed him Apollo
And you received second sight
You received clues in the night
And you gave mortals your holy light
A light to help them see
All that would come to be

And the days were filled by Apollo's Sun
And the dark of night gave everyone

Visions and omens and prophecies
All mortals could scry through the darkest sky
To see visions and omens and prophecies
All mortals could hear the hiss of the whispers
Telling of Fortune and Fate
Until Apollo took back each prophecy
And once again gave us mystery
So now all mortals will forever be
Lost and waiting for divinity
For now Apollo holds tight
To the gift of second sight

Oh Apollo
Great Apollo
God of the Sun and Prophecy
The golden god
Like the golden Sun
Giving light so that mortals can see
Giving light from each prophecy
Giving light so that mortals can see
What will come to be
What will come to be

(MESSENGER *enters.*)

MESSENGER:
You temple guardians and sentries near
The altar, is the King among you here
Beyond these guarded gates? Go call within
For our great ruler.

LEADER OF THE CHORUS:
But may I begin
To speak without permission? Tell me what
Is happening.

MESSENGER:
The two young men have cut
Loose from their bonds, and they were aided by
The spawn of Agamemnon. She is why

They now escape from here while carrying
The image of the Goddess. And they bring
It back to Greece within the hull of their
Great ship.

LEADER OF THE CHORUS:

So unbelievable they dare
It! But the one you seek has gone away.
He left the temple in great haste.

MESSENGER:

You say
He left? But where? He truly needs to know
What happened.

LEADER OF THE CHORUS:

We were not informed. But go
Right after him outside and find him. Then
You can recount it all to him.

MESSENGER:

And when
I see how you respond I surely know
That women can't be trusted. And you show
Me that you had a hand in this.

LEADER OF THE CHORUS:

Are you
A madman? Tell me what we have to do
With flights of foreigners? Now you should bring
This far beyond our gate and to the King.

MESSENGER:

I will the moment I can guarantee
By hearing it from other lips that he
Is not within.
(He calls out:)

Hello in there. Can you
Unlock the doors? As I am burdened to
Inform the King of dreadful news.

(THOAS *re-enters with* GUARDS.)

THOAS:

You dare
Disturb the temple of the Goddess? There
Outside while striking at the gates? And who
Are you to send this noise and fear all through
The sacred temple?

MESSENGER:

All these women lied
And told me plainly you were far outside
These walls. They tried to send me far away,
And yet it seems that you are here.

THOAS:

And they
Expected what advantage from this ruse?

MESSENGER:

I will tell all, but first, I fear we lose
Advantage with each passing moment as
The virgin priestess just escaped. She has
Absconded with the foreigners and takes
The sacred statue with her. She forsakes
All truth in name of foul deceit and lies.

THOAS:

What do you say? Some force could compromise
Her?

MESSENGER:

It is much to be believed. It was
Orestes that she rescued.

THOAS:

But how does
The son of Clytemnestra figure in
This?

MESSENGER:
He's the very one they held within
For sacrifice to Artemis.

THOAS:
Great Gods!
There are no words for this; what are the odds
That this could be?

MESSENGER:
You must not ponder how
But wonder why. The facts will then allow
You to devise a plan to go pursue
These foreigners.

THOAS:
I listen now as you
Have proven that your words are worthy. I
Suspect they cannot travel far, and my
Great fleet and spears will soon pursue them.

MESSENGER:
We

All came upon the shore beside the sea
Where young Orestes had his ship, although
We did not know that it was there. And so
When Agamemnon's daughter signaled we
Were to remain behind, though faithfully,
We still had both of them in chains. But then
She freed them of their chains and told the men
To walk away from her and who she held
As prisoners. So we stood back, compelled
To think that she would speak a sacred rite
That was not for our ears. We saw the sight
Of her directing both of them, their chains
Within her hand behind them, but no reins
On them. It seemed suspicious, but we let
Them walk ahead. It seemed the sun would set
Before we heard another sound, but through

The silence she let out a shout. We knew
That she was conjuring and cast a spell
To cleanse them both of murder. It went well
Beyond an hour, and we worried she
Could not control these foreigners set free
And they might murder her and flee. But still
We feared to interrupt her chants until
The ritual was over. So we sat
There silent with resolve while hoping that
We soon could intervene. But then we spied
A great Greek ship with rowers on each side,
And both the foreigners were at the stern
And free of bonds or chains. We had concern
To see the crew move quickly to prepare
The ship to sail. The sails flew in the air
As cables pulled and ladders lowered to
Allow the priestess on the ship. We threw
Ourselves without a hesitation in
The sea. We saw the foreigners begin
To take the priestess and the statue, so
We grabbed their oars and cables. "Do you know
What you dare do?" We called at them, "You take
A Priestess, and you make a great mistake.
That statue is a holy relic; you
Would dare remove it from our land? And who
Are you descended from that you would dare
To do this?" And he said, "I am the heir
Of Agamemnon. You may know my name:
Orestes! And this priestess has the same
Great lineage as me as she is my
Own sister. And I now will take her by
This ship across the sea to home." But we
Would not relent and grabbed her violently
To bring her back to you. And so they struck
Us hard across our faces. It was luck
Or Fate that they did not have swords. But we
Were not armed either. But still, rapidly

Our fists were flying, feet were kicking out
And landing on our torsos with a shout.
And soon all were exhausted, so we fled
Up to a nearby cliff as we all bled
From gashes on our heads and eyes. But we
Were soon upon the cliff and cleverly
We started hurling stones at them. But then
Their archers all appeared on deck and when
They fired arrows, we all ran away.
But then a giant wave appeared and they
Were shocked to find they almost ran aground.
The priestess screamed in fear. She made a sound
That made her brother jump into the sea
And hoist her on his shoulder. And then he
Climbed up the ladder to the ship and set
Her there and placed the statue by her. Wet
And bleeding, then Orestes shouted to
His men, "Now sailors, grab the oars and through
Your strength we shove the shore away. We make
The water white with foam and stir the wake
As we sail forth. We have succeeded, men.
We have the treasure that we sought out when
We dared to test the clashing stones!" They yelled
Out shouts and hoisted as the ocean swelled,
But once they left the harbor, how the tide
Grew angry and it pushed them back inside
The inlet. Though they fought it with each oar,
It pressed them quickly back against the shore.
Then Agamemnon's daughter made a cry
And raised her voice while calling to the sky,
"Great Artemis, I am your priestess. Take
Me from this land and send me home. Forsake
Us if you must if you cannot forgive
The theft of me. But I know that you live
With great love for your brother as do I."
The sailors started singing to the sky
And prayed as well and dug their oars within

The deep, dark water while all joining in
The music of the song. They did not make
It. They are in the rocks within the wake
Of angry water. They are trapped as they
Pull sails and ropes in hopes to get away,
And I was sent to you, my King, to tell
You what is trapped within the sea's great swell.
I say take ropes and chains down to the shore,
And if the sea does not hold back its roar,
Then they should not escape to safety. As
Poseidon rules the oceans and he has
Protected Troy, there is no way that he
Will let the spawn of Agamemnon be
Set free. They are a gift to you, and they
Are in your grasp. And she forgets the day
In Aulis as a sacrifice and how
The Goddess rescued her. She broke her vow.

LEADER OF THE CHORUS:
Oh poor Iphigenia, you will be
Beside your brother, but your destiny
Is death should you be taken back before
Our lord and King.

(THOAS *calls out to his guards who exit during the
following:*)

THOAS:
             And now down to the shore,
My loyal Taurians! Hold to the rein
You place upon your horse. We will contain
The Grecian ships within our harbor. Now
We call the Goddess forth and make a vow
To hunt these blasphemers. By land and sea
We will attack, so board the ships as we
Will take them from each side. And leave no one
Alive. Hurl them upon the rocks or run
Your spears into their bodies.

(He addresses CHORUS*:)*
                                        As for you,
Foul women who conspired with them: Do
You think I will not punish you? When we
Are not preoccupied with treason, see
How quickly I remember what you did.

(The GODDESS ATHENA *appears from above.)*

                              ATHENA:
But will you dare to do what I forbid?
King Thoas, why do you send off your men
In mad pursuit? All words have value when
Athena has arrived. So hold your rage
And all your soldiers. Do not dare engage
Them, as Orestes was inspired through
An oracle sent by Apollo to
Relieve him of the Furies' battle cry
And also to redeem his father by
Retrieving his lost sister and then take
A statue of my sister. This will break
The Furies' hold on him. I speak to you,
King Thoas: I know what you mean to do
By striking down Orestes on the sea.
But now Poseidon holds his wrath for me.
And so the water sits as still as glass.
(She calls out:)
Now hear the sound of my commands. Now pass
Beyond these walls and to the sea: Hear me
Orestes! I am here though you can't see
Me. Take your sister and the statue to
The God-constructed Athens, and then you
Must go beyond its borders. Seek to find
The sacred rocks where ridges are defined.
And that, Orestes, is where you will build
A temple. See your destiny fulfilled,
As when the very statue that you hold
Is placed within it. Let the tale be told

Of how it came from Tauric lands and how
You dared retrieve it. And we must allow
The tale of all your many sufferings
To be repeated as the temple brings
The worshipers of Artemis to pray
Each year at a great festival. And say
That she was Goddess of the Tauric land.
And then decree a festival be planned
To celebrate her every year. See that
A sword is sharpened and positioned at
A man's unguarded neck. And let them cut
It closely so it only trickles, but
One drop enough to make you feel relief
That you were spared and rescued from your grief.
Then praise the Goddess Artemis and say
That she be honored on this holy day.
And then, Iphigenia, you will be
Her priestess once again and hold the key
To her most-holy shrine. And you shall stay
There as a guardian until the day
You die. And they will bury you within
The finest woven robes with honor. In
This temple there are women seeking to
Return to Greece. I say, Orestes, you
Are charged to see them safely there as I
Have saved you once before. Remember my
Swift intervention saved you on the day
You had your trial. So save them. Away
With you, last son of Atreus, and take
Your sister home to safety.
(*She addresses* THOAS:)

                       Do not make
An angry stance at this King Thoas.

                       THOAS:
                            I
Know well, Athena, mortals dare not try

To disobey a god's command. I say
It is unwise. And so there is no way
I will be angry at Orestes for
Absconding with the holy statue or
Recovering his sister. What could I
Dare do to fight the Gods? So let them fly
Back to their homeland with the statue to
Enshrine it as you ordered. Just as you
Have ordered all these women should go free
To Greece. And be assured that I will see
My army lay their weapons down, and my
Great ships will not impede them. I will try
To do as you see fit, oh Goddess.

ATHENA:
You

Are most commended. Know that it is true
Of gods and mortals that necessity
Can rule us all.
(She calls out:)

Now, wind upon the sea:

Take Agamemnon's children home at last,
So far beyond the horrors of the past
As I accompany the image of
My sister. Mortals, hail the Gods above!

(ATHENA *disappears and* THOAS *exits.*)

CHORUS:

Yes Athena
Great Athena
Revered among mortals
And immortals
We now go across the sea
Knowing that you will always be
Above
You hear us sing
As we sing your praise
As we sing your song

We carry out your every command
As you take us back to our land
To our land that we love
(Begins to exit in a procession)

I am a bird   May I fly beyond this place
Who can freely sing   May I fly across the sea
I am a bird   May I follow Apollo
Who now will fly   As he takes the Sun
Over the rocks   Far across the sea

Oh I could sing   May the sheerest veil
Of a land far away   Cover my hair
Oh I could sing   May I be married
And raise my voice   Where I once was a maiden
To Artemis   Back in Greece
Artemis Artemis   Back in Greece
And call her name
But now once again at
  home
Praying to her   May I dance about
By the palm trees and
  laurel
Calling to her   Like the girl that I once was
By the vine-ripened olive
Singing to her   Back in Greece
Like a ripple on water   Back in Greece
Like the singing of a swan
Back in Greece
Back in Greece

(CHORUS *exits.*)

END OF PLAY

9 798888 560273